FOUR
SEASONS
FIVE
SENSES

FOUR SEASONS FIVE SENSES

POEMS SELECTED BY
ELINOR PARKER

ILLUSTRATED BY DIANE DeGROAT

CHARLES SCRIBNER'S SONS
NEW YORK

BOOKS BY ELINOR PARKER

COOKING FOR ONE

SOME DOGS

ENTERTAINING SINGLEHANDED

MOST GRACIOUS MAJESTY

ANTHOLOGIES

A BIRTHDAY GARLAND

100 STORY POEMS

100 POEMS ABOUT PEOPLE

I WAS JUST THINKING

100 MORE STORY POEMS

THE SINGING AND THE GOLD

POEMS OF WILLIAM WORDSWORTH
(CROWELL POETS SERIES)

HERE AND THERE:
100 POEMS ABOUT PLACES

1 3 5 7 9 11 13 15 17 19 V/C 20 18 16 14 12 10 8 6 4 2

Printed in the United States of America
Library of Congress Catalog Card Number 73-14402
ISBN 0-684-13661-9

ACKNOWLEDGMENTS

The Editor and the Publisher gratefully acknowledge the following poets, agents, and publishers for permission to reprint poems in this anthology. Every effort has been made to locate all persons having any rights or interests in the material published here. If some acknowledgments have not been made, their omission is unintentional and is regretted.

"The Burning of the Leaves" by Laurence Binyon: Reprinted by permission of Mrs. Nicolete Gray and The Society of Authors, on behalf of the Laurence Binyon Estate.

"London Snow," "North Wind in October," and "Spring Goeth All in White" by Robert Bridges: From *The Shorter Poems of Robert Bridges*. Reprinted by permission of The Clarendon Press, Oxford.

"Fall, Leaves, Fall," "How Still, How Happy," and "The Night-Wind" by Emily Jane Brontë: From *The Complete Poems of Emily Jane Brontë*, ed. by C. W. Hatfield. Reprinted by permission of Columbia University Press.

"The Secret" by Robert P. Tristram Coffin: Reprinted with permission of Macmillan Publishing Co., Inc. from *Saltwater Farm* by Robert P. Tristram Coffin. Copyright 1935 by Macmillan Publishing Co., Inc., renewed 1963 by Margaret Coffin Halvosa.

"The Rain" and "Rich Days" by W. H. Davies: From *Complete Poems of W. H. Davies*. Copyright © 1963 by Jonathan Cape Ltd. Reprinted by permission of Jonathan Cape Ltd. and Wesleyan University Press.

"The Snow-flake" by Walter de la Mare: From *The Complete Poems of Walter de la Mare* 1970. Reprinted by permission of The Literary Trustees of Walter de la Mare, and The Society of Authors as their representative.

"A Light Exists in Spring," "As Imperceptibly as Grief," "Dear March, Come In!" "The Morns Are Meeker Than They Were," "The Sky is Low, the Clouds are Mean," "There's a Certain Slant of Light," "These Are the Days When Birds Come Back," by Emily Dickinson: Reprinted by permission of Little, Brown and Company and the Trustees of Amherst College from Thomas H.

CONTENTS

FROM **FROST AT MIDNIGHT**

Therefore all seasons shall be sweet to thee,
Whether the summer clothe the general earth
With greenness, or the redbreast sit and sing
Betwixt the tufts of snow on the bare branch
Of mossy apple-tree, while the nigh thatch
Smokes in the sun-thaw; whether the eave-drops fall
Heard only in the trances of the blast,
Or if the secret ministry of frost
Shall hang them up in silent icicles,
Quietly shining to the quiet Moon.

SAMUEL TAYLOR COLERIDGE

WINTER

SONNET

The weary year his race now having run,
    The new begins his compassed course anew:
With shew of morning mild he hath begun,
    Betokening peace and plenty to ensue.
    So let us, which this change of weather view,
Change eke[†] our minds and former lives amend;
    The old year's sins forepast let us eschew,
And fly the faults with which we did offend.
Then shall the new year's joy forth freshly send
    Into the glooming world his gladsome ray;
And all these storms, which now his beauty blend,
    Shall turn to calms and timely clear away.
        So likewise, love, cheer you your heavy spright,
        And change old year's annoy to new delight.

EDMUND SPENSER

[†]*also*

3

BLOW, BLOW, THOU WINTER WIND

Blow, blow, thou winter wind,
Thou art not so unkind
   As man's ingratitude:
Thy tooth is not so keen,
Because thou art not seen,
   Although thy breath be rude.
Heigh ho! sing, heigh ho! unto the green holly:
Most friendship is feigning, most loving mere folly:
   Then heigh ho the holly!
   This life is most jolly.

Freeze, freeze, thou bitter sky,
That dost not bite so nigh
   As benefits forgot:
Though thou the waters warp,
Thy sting is not so sharp
   As friend remember'd not.
Heigh ho! sing, heigh ho! unto the green holly:
Most friendship is feigning, most loving mere folly:
   Then heigh ho the holly!
   This life is most jolly.

WILLIAM SHAKESPEARE

WINTER

When icicles hang by the wall,
    And Dick the shepherd blows his nail,
And Tom bears logs into the hall,
    And milk comes frozen home in pail,
When blood is nipped and ways be foul,
Then nightly sings the staring owl,
               To-whit!
To-who!—a merry note,
While greasy Joan doth keel the pot.

When all aloud the wind doth blow,
    And coughing drowns the parson's saw,
And birds sit brooding in the snow,
    And Marian's nose looks red and raw,
When roasted crabs hiss in the bowl,
Then nightly sings the staring owl,
               To-whit!
To-who!—a merry note,
While greasy Joan doth keel the pot.

WILLIAM SHAKESPEARE

FROM **SNOW-BOUND**

The sun that brief December day
Rose cheerless over hills of gray,
And, darkly circled, gave at noon
A sadder light than waning moon.
Slow tracing down the thickening sky
Its mute and ominous prophecy,
A portent seeming less than threat,
It sank from sight before it set.
A chill no coat, however stout,
Of homespun stuff could quite shut out,
A hard, dull bitterness of cold,
That checked, mid-vein, the circling race
Of life-blood in the sharpened face,
The coming of the snow-storm told.
The wind blew east: we heard the roar
Of Ocean on his wintry shore,
And felt the strong pulse throbbing there
Beat with low rhythm our inland air.

*   *   *   *   *

Unwarmed by any sunset light
The gray day darkened into night,
A night made hoary with the swarm
And whirl-dance of the blinding storm,
As zigzag quavering to and fro
Crossed and recrossed the wingèd snow:
And ere the early bedtime came
The white drift piled the window-frame,
And through the glass the clothes-line posts
Looked in like tall and sheeted ghosts.

So all night long the storm roared on:
The morning broke without a sun;
In tiny spherule traced with lines
Of Nature's geometric signs,
In starry flake and pellicle,
All day the hoary meteor fell;
And when the second morning shone,
We looked upon a world unknown,
On nothing we could call our own.
Around the glistening wonder bent
The blue walls of the firmament,
No cloud above, no earth below,—
A universe of sky and snow!
The old familiar sights of ours
Took marvellous shapes: strange domes and towers
Rose up where sty or corn-crib stood,
On garden-wall or belt of wood;
A smooth white mound the brush-pile showed,
A fenceless drift what once was road;
The bridle-post an old man sat
With loose-flung coat and high cocked hat;
The well-curb had a Chinese roof;
And even the long sweep, high aloof,
In its slant splendor, seemed to tell
Of Pisa's living miracle.

JOHN GREENLEAF WHITTIER

THE SNOW-STORM

Announced by all the trumpets of the sky,
Arrives the snow, and, driving o'er the fields,
Seems nowhere to alight: the whited air
Hides hills and woods, the river, and the heaven,
And veils the farm-house at the garden's end.
The sled and traveller stopped, the courier's feet
Delayed, all friends shut out, the housemates sit
Around the radiant fireplace, enclosed
In a tumultuous privacy of storm.

Come see the north wind's masonry.
Out of an unseen quarry evermore
Furnished with tile, the fierce artificer
Curves his white bastions with projected roof
Round every windward stake, or tree, or door.
Speeding, the myriad-handed, his wild work
So fanciful, so savage, nought cares he
For number or proportion. Mockingly,
On coop or kennel he hangs Parian wreaths;
A swan-like form invests the hidden thorn;
Fills up the farmer's lane from wall to wall,
Maugre[†] the farmer's sighs; and at the gate
A tapering turret overtops the work.
And when his hours are numbered, and the world
Is all his own, retiring, as he were not,
Leaves, when the sun appears, astonished art
To mimic in slow structures, stone by stone,
Built in an age, the mad wind's night-work,
The frolic architecture of the snow.

RALPH WALDO EMERSON

[†]*in spite of*

WINTER

Now Winter as a shrivelled scroll
    Casts the rags of Summer away,
Naked and beautiful the stripped soul
    Haunts the bare woods, austere and grey.

Clean in the quiet hour she goes
    She has renounced the lure of sense,
More beautiful than the gold and rose
    In her thin veil of innocence.

White as the snow she walks the woods,
    More beautiful than the joyous Spring;
Scourged of the winds and washed by floods,
    Spirit and flame, with a drooped wing.

There is not a stain in this pale light,
    The new-washed skies, the tonic air,
She, the moon's sister, walks the height,
    A spiritual beauty past compare.

When all the Summer world is dust
    And Autumn glories fallen to clay,
This soul of beauty, chill, august,
    Wanders by wood and waterway.

KATHARINE TYNAN

And in the frosty season, when the sun
Was set, and visible for many a mile
The cottage windows blazed through twilight gloom,
I heeded not their summons: happy time
It was indeed for all of us—for me
It was a time of rapture! Clear and loud
The village clock tolled six,—I wheeled about,
Proud and exulting like an untired horse
That cares not for his home. All shod with steel,
We hissed along the polished ice in games
Confederate, imitative of the chase
And woodland pleasures,—the resounding horn,
The pack loud chiming, and the hunted hare.
So through the darkness and the cold we flew,
And not a voice was idle; with the din
Smitten, the precipices rang aloud;
The leafless trees and every icy crag
Tinkled like iron; while far distant hills
Into the tumult sent an alien sound
Of melancholy not unnoticed, while the stars
Eastward were sparkling clear, and in the west
The orange sky of evening died away.
Not seldom from the uproar I retired
Into a silent bay, or sportively
Glanced sideway, leaving the tumultuous throng,
To cut across the reflex of a star
That fled, and, flying still before me, gleamed
Upon the glassy plain; and oftentimes
When we had given our bodies to the wind,
And all the shadowy banks on either side
Came sweeping through the darkness, spinning still

The rapid line of motion, then at once
Have I, reclining back upon my heels,
Stopped short; yet still the solitary cliffs
Wheeled by me—even as if the earth had rolled
With visible motion her diurnal round!
Behind me they did stretch in solemn train,
Feebler and feebler, and I stood and watched
Till all was tranquil as a dreamless sleep.

WILLIAM WORDSWORTH

DIRGE FOR THE YEAR

Orphan hours, the year is dead,
    Come and sigh, come and weep!
Merry hours, smile instead,
    For the year is but asleep.
See, it smiles as it is sleeping,
Mocking your untimely weeping.

As an earthquake rocks a corse
    In its coffin in the clay,
So White Winter, that rough nurse,
    Rocks the death-cold year today;
Solemn hours! wait aloud
For your mother in her shroud.

As the wild air stirs and sways
    The tree-swung cradle of a child,
So the breath of these rude days
    Rocks the year:—be calm and mild,
Trembling hours, she will arise
With new love within her eyes.

January grey is here,
    Like a sexton by her grave:
February bears the bier,
    March with grief doth howl and rave,
And April weeps—but, O ye hours,
Follow with May's fairest flowers.

PERCY BYSSHE SHELLEY

THERE'S A CERTAIN
SLANT OF LIGHT

There's a certain slant of light,
On winter afternoons,
That oppresses, like the weight
Of cathedral tunes.

Heavenly hurt it gives us;
We can find no scar,
But internal difference
Where the meanings are.

None may teach it anything,
'Tis the seal despair,—
An imperial affliction
Sent us of the air.

When it comes, the landscape listens,
Shadows hold their breath;
When it goes, 'tis like the distance
On the look of death.

                    EMILY DICKINSON

THE SKY IS LOW,
THE CLOUDS ARE MEAN

The sky is low, the clouds are mean,
A travelling flake of snow
Across a barn or through a rut
Debates if it will go.

A narrow wind complains all day
How some one treated him;
Nature, like us, is sometimes caught
Without her diadem.

EMILY DICKINSON

WINTER

The frost is here,
And fuel is dear,
And woods are sear,
And fires burn clear,
And frost is here
And has bitten the heel of the going year.

Bite, frost, bite!
You roll up away from the light
The blue wood-louse, and the plump dormouse,
And the bees are still'd, and the flies are kill'd,
And you bite far into the heart of the house,
But not into mine.

Bite, frost, bite!
The woods are all the searer,
The fuel is all the dearer,
The fires are all the clearer,
My spring is all the nearer,
You have bitten into the heart of the earth,
But not into mine.

ALFRED TENNYSON

HOW STILL, HOW HAPPY

How still, how happy! Those are words
That once would scarce agree together;
I loved the plashing of the surge,
The changing heaven, the breezy weather,

More than smooth seas and cloudless skies
And solemn, soothing, softened airs
That in the forest woke no sighs
And from the green spray shook no tears.

How still, how happy! Now I feel
Where silence dwells is sweeter far
Than laughing mirth's most joyous swell
However pure its raptures are.

Come, sit down on this sunny stone:
'Tis wintry light o'er flowerless moors—
But sit—for we are all alone
And clear expand heaven's breathless shores.

I could think in the withered grass
Spring's budding wreaths we might discern;
The violet's eye might shyly flash
And young leaves shoot among the fern.

It is but thought—full many a night
The snow shall clothe those hills afar
And stars shall add a drearier blight
And winds shall wage a wilder war,

Before the lark may herald in
Fresh foliage twined with blossoms fair

And summer days again begin
Their glory-haloed crown to wear.

Yet my heart loves December's smile
As much as July's golden beam;
Then let us sit and watch the while
The blue ice curdling on the stream.

EMILY BRONTË

THE DARKLING THRUSH

I leant upon a coppice gate
    When Frost was spectre-gray,
And Winter's dregs made desolate
    The weakening eye of day.
The tangled bine-stems† scored the sky
    Like strings of broken lyres,
And all mankind that haunted nigh
    Had sought their household fires.

The land's sharp features seemed to be
    The Century's corpse outleant,
His crypt the cloudy canopy,
    The wind his death-lament.
The ancient pulse of germ and birth
    Was shrunken hard and dry,
And every spirit upon earth
    Seemed fervourless as I.

At once a voice arose among
    The bleak twigs overhead
In a full-hearted evensong
    Of joy illimited;
An aged thrush, frail, gaunt, and small,
    In blast beruffled plume,
Had chosen thus to fling his soul
    Upon the growing gloom.

So little cause for carolings
    Of such ecstatic sound

†woodbine, a European twining shrub

Was written on terrestrial things
    Afar or nigh around,
That I could think there trembled through
    His happy good-night air
Some blessed Hope, whereof he knew
    And I was unaware.

THOMAS HARDY

LONDON SNOW

When men were all asleep the snow came flying,
In large white flakes falling on the city brown,
Stealthily and perpetually settling and loosely lying,
    Hushing the latest traffic of the drowsy town;
Deadening, muffling, stifling its murmurs failing;
Lazily and incessantly floating down and down:
    Silently sifting and veiling road, roof and railing;
Hiding difference, making unevenness even,
Into angles and crevices softly drifting and sailing.
    All night it fell, and when full inches seven
It lay in the depth of its uncompacted lightness,
The clouds blew off from a high and frosty heaven;
    And all woke earlier for the unaccustomed brightness
Of the winter dawning, the strange unheavenly glare:
The eye marvelled—marvelled at the dazzling whiteness;
    The ear hearkened to the stillness of the solemn air;
No sound of wheel rumbling nor of foot falling,
And the busy morning cries came thin and spare.
    Then boys I heard, as they went to school, calling,
They gathered up the crystal manna to freeze
Their tongues with tasting, the hands with snowballing;
    Or rioted in a drift, plunging up to the knees;
Or peering up from under the white-mossed wonder,
'O look at the trees!' they cried, 'O look at the trees!'
    With lessened load a few carts creak and blunder,
Following along the white deserted way,
A country company long dispersed asunder:
    When now already the sun, in pale display

Standing by Paul's high dome, spread forth below
His sparkling beams, and awoke the stir of the day.
　　For now doors open, and war is waged with the snow;
And trains of sombre men, past tale of number,
Tread long brown paths, as toward their toil they go:
　　But even for them awhile no cares encumber
Their minds diverted; the daily word is unspoken,
The daily thoughts of labour and sorrow slumber
At the sight of the beauty that greets them,
　　For the charm they have broken.

ROBERT BRIDGES

DUST OF SNOW

The way a crow
Shook down on me
The dust of snow
From a hemlock tree

Has given my heart
A change of mood
And saved some part
Of a day I had rued.

ROBERT FROST

STOPPING BY WOODS
ON A SNOWY EVENING

Whose woods these are I think I know.
His house is in the village, though;
He will not see me stopping here
To watch his woods fill up with snow.

My little horse must think it queer
To stop without a farmhouse near
Between the woods and frozen lake
The darkest evening of the year.

He gives his harness bells a shake
To ask if there is some mistake.
The only other sound's the sweep
Of easy wind and downy flake.

The woods are lovely, dark, and deep.
But I have promises to keep,
And miles to go before I sleep,
And miles to go before I sleep.

ROBERT FROST

VELVET SHOES

Let us walk in the white snow
    In a soundless space;
With footsteps quiet and slow,
    At a tranquil pace,
    Under veils of white lace.

I shall go shod in silk,
    And you in wool,
White as a white cow's milk,
    More beautiful
    Than the breast of a gull.

We shall walk through the still town
    In a windless peace;
We shall step upon white down,
    Upon silver fleece,
    Upon softer than these.

We shall walk in velvet shoes:
    Wherever we go
Silence will fall like dews
    On white silence below.
    We shall walk in the snow.

ELINOR WYLIE

SING A SONG OF HONEY

Honey from the white rose, honey from the red,
Is not that a pretty thing to spread upon your bread!
When the flower is open, the bee begins to buzz,
I'm very glad, I'm very glad, I'm very glad it does—
Honey from the lily,
     Honey from the May[†],
And the daffodilly,
     And the lilac spray—
When the snow is falling, when the fires are red,
Is not that a pretty thing to spread upon your bread?

Honey from the heather, honey from the lime,
Is not that a dainty thing to eat in winter-time?
Honey from the cherry, honey from the ling,
Honey from the celandine that opens in the Spring.
Honey from the clover,
     Honey from the pear—
Summer may be over,
     But I shall never care.
When the fires are blazing, honey from the lime
Makes a very dainty dish to eat in winter-time.

Kings will leave their counting any time they're told
Queens are in the parlor spreading honey gold,
Gold from honeysuckle, gold from lupins' spire—
Who will stay in counting-house and miss the parlour fire?

[†] *a spring-flowering shrub*

Honey from the daisy,
    Honey from the plum,
Kings will all be lazy,
    And glad that Winter's come.
Who will keep to counting till the sum is told?
I'll be in the parlour and eating honey-gold.

BARBARA EUPHAN TODD

SOFT SNOW

I walked abroad on a snowy day:
I ask'd the soft snow with me to play:
She play'd and she melted in all her prime,
And the winter call'd it a dreadful crime.

WILLIAM BLAKE

SNOW-FLAKES

Out of the bosom of the air,
    Out of the cloud-folds of her garments shaken,
Over the woodlands brown and bare,
    Over the harvest-fields forsaken,
        Silent, and soft, and slow
        Descends the snow.

Even as our cloudy fancies take
    Suddenly shape in some divine expression,
Even as the troubled heart doth make
    In the white countenance confession,
        The troubled sky reveals
        The grief it feels.

This is the poem of the air,
    Slowly in silent syllables recorded;
This is the secret of despair,
    Long in its cloudy bosom hoarded,
        Now whispered and revealed
        To wood and field.

HENRY WADSWORTH LONGFELLOW

TO A SNOW-FLAKE

What heart could have thought you?—
Past our devisal
(O filigree petal!)
Fashioned so purely,
Fragilely, surely,
From what Paradisal
Imagineless metal
Too costly for cost?
Who hammered you, wrought you,
From argentine vapour?—
'God was my shaper.
Passing surmisal,
He hammered, He wrought me,
From curled silver vapour,
To lust of His mind:—
Thou couldst not have thought me!
So purely, so palely,
Tinily, surely,
Mightily, frailly,
Insculped and embossed,
With His hammer of wind,
And His graver of frost.'

FRANCIS THOMPSON

THE SNOW-FLAKE

Before I melt,
Come, look at me!
This lovely icy filigree!
Of a great forest
In one night
I make a wilderness
Of white:
By skyey cold
Of crystals made,
All softly, on
Your finger laid,
I pause, that you
My beauty see:
Breathe, and I vanish
Instantly.

WALTER DE LA MARE

THE NEW MOON
FROM DEJECTION: AN ODE

For lo! the new Moon winter-bright!
And overspread with phantom light
(With swimming phantom light o'erspread
But rimm'd and circled by a silver thread),
I see the old Moon in her lap, foretelling
  The coming on of rain and squally blast.
And oh! that even now the gust were swelling,
  And the slant night-shower driving loud and fast.

   SAMUEL TAYLOR COLERIDGE

NIGHT

Stars over snow
  And in the west a planet
Swinging below a star—
  Look for a lovely thing and you will find it,
It is not far—
  It never will be far.

   SARA TEASDALE

STAR-TALK

'Are you awake, Gemelli,
    This frosty night?'
'We'll be awake till reveillé,
Which is Sunrise,' say the Gemelli,
'It's no good trying to go to sleep:
If there's wine to be got we'll drink it deep,
    But rest is hopeless tonight,
    But rest is hopeless tonight.'

'Are you cold too, poor Pleiads,
    This frosty night?'
'Yes, and so are the Hyads:
See us cuddle and hug,' say the Pleiads,
'All six in a ring: it keeps us warm:
We huddle together like birds in a storm:
    It's bitter weather tonight,
    It's bitter weather tonight.'

'What do you hunt, Orion,
    This starry night?'
'The Ram, the Bull, and the Lion,
And the Great Bear,' says Orion,
'With my starry quiver and beautiful belt
I am trying to find a good thick pelt
    To warm my shoulders tonight,
    To warm my shoulders tonight.'

'Did you hear that, Great She-bear,
    This frosty night?'
'Yes, he's talking of stripping *me* bare
Of my own big fur,' says the She-bear,

'I'm afraid of the man and his terrible arrow:
The thought of it chills my bones to the marrow,
 And the frost so cruel tonight!
 And the frost so cruel tonight!'

'How is your trade, Aquarius,
 This frosty night?'
'Complaints is many and various
And my feet are cold,' says Aquarius,
'There's Venus objects to dolphin-scales,
And Mars to Crab-spawn found in my pails,
 And the pump has frozen tonight,
 And the pump has frozen tonight.'

ROBERT GRAVES

SPRING

THE SNOWDROP

Many, many welcomes
February fair-maid,
Ever as of old time,
Solitary firstling,
Coming in the cold time,
Prophet of the gay time,
Prophet of the May time,
Prophet of the roses,
Many, many welcomes
February fair-maid!

ALFRED TENNYSON

SPRING

> Sound the Flute!
> Now it's mute.
> Birds delight
> Day and Night;
> Nightingale
> In the dale,
> Lark in Sky,
> Merrily,
Merrily, Merrily, to welcome in the Year.

> Little Boy,
> Full of joy;
> Little Girl,
> Sweet and small;
> Cock does crow,
> So do you;
> Merry voice,
> Infant noise.
Merrily, Merrily, to welcome in the Year.

> Little Lamb,
> Here I am;
> Come and lick
> My white neck;
> Let me pull
> Your soft Wool;
> Let me kiss
> Your soft face:
Merrily, Merrily, to welcome in the Year.

WILLIAM BLAKE

THE ECHOING GREEN

The Sun does arise,
And make happy the skies;
The merry bells ring
To welcome the Spring;
The skylark and thrush,
The birds of the bush,
Sing louder around
To the bells' cheerful sound,
While our sports shall be seen
On the Echoing Green.

Old John, with white hair,
Does laugh away care,
Sitting under the oak,
Among the old folk,
They laugh at our play,
And soon they all say:
"Such, such were the joys
"When we all, girls and boys,
"In our youth time were seen
"On the Echoing Green."

Till the little ones, weary,
No more can be merry;
The sun does descend,
And our sports have an end.
Round the laps of their mothers
Many sisters and brothers,
Like birds in their nest,
Are ready for rest,

And sport no more seen
On the darkening Green.

WILLIAM BLAKE

TO DAFFADILLS

Faire daffadills, we weep to see
      You haste away so soone:
As yet the early-rising Sun
        Has not attain'd his Noone.
              Stay, stay,
            Until the hasting day
              Has run
            But to the Even-song;
And having pray'd together, wee
        Will goe with you along.

We have short time to stay, as you,
      We have as short a Spring;
As quick a growth to meet Decay,
        As you or any thing.
            We die,
          As your hours doe, and drie
            Away,
          Like to the Summers raine;
Or as the pearles of Mornings dew
        Ne'er to be found again.

ROBERT HERRICK

SPRING

When daisies pied and violets blue,
    And lady-smocks all silver-white,
And cuckoo-buds of yellow hue
    Do paint the meadows with delight,
The cuckoo then, on every tree,
Mocks married men; for thus sings he,
            Cuckoo!
Cuckoo, cuckoo!— O word of fear,
Unpleasing to a married ear!

When shepherds pipe on oaten straws,
    And merry larks are ploughmen's clocks,
And turtles† tread, and rooks, and daws,
    And maidens bleach their summer smocks
The cuckoo then, on every tree,
Mocks married men; for thus sings he,
            Cuckoo!
Cuckoo, cuckoo!— O word of fear,
Unpleasing to a married ear!

WILLIAM SHAKESPEARE

†*turtledoves*

Now fades the last long streak of snow,
    Now burgeons every maze of quick†
    About the flowering squares, and thick
By ashen roots the violets blow.

Now rings the woodland loud and long,
    The distance takes a lovelier hue,
    And drown'd in yonder living blue
The lark becomes a sightless song.

Now dance the lights on lawn and lea,
    The flocks are whiter down the vale,
    And milkier every milky sail
On winding stream or distant sea.

Where now the seamew pipes, or dives
    In yonder greening gleam, and fly
    The happy birds, that change their sky
To build and brood; that live their lives

From land to land; and in my breast
    Spring wakens too; and my regret
    Becomes an April violet,
And buds and blossoms like the rest.

ALFRED TENNYSON

†*a European grass*

DEAR MARCH, COME IN!

Dear March, come in!
How glad I am!
I looked for you before.
Put down your hat—
You must have walked—
How out of breath you are!
Dear March, how are you?
And the rest?
Did you leave Nature well?
Oh, March, come right upstairs with me,
I have so much to tell!

I got your letter, and the bird's;
The maples never knew
That you were coming,—I declare,
How red their faces grew!
But, March, forgive me—
And all those hills
You left for me to hue;
There was no purple suitable
You took it all with you.

Who knocks? That April!
Lock the door!
I will not be pursued!
He stayed away a year, to call
When I am occupied.
But trifles look so trivial
As soon as you have come,

That blame is just as dear a praise
And praise as mere as blame.

EMILY DICKINSON

A LIGHT EXISTS IN SPRING

A light exists in spring
    Not present on the year
At any other period.
    When March is scarcely here

A color stands abroad
    On solitary hills
That science cannot overtake,
    But human nature *feels*.

It waits upon the lawn;
    It shows the furthest tree
Upon the furthest slope we know;
    It almost speaks to me.

Then, as horizons step,
    Or noons report away,
Without the formula of sound,
    It passes, and we stay.

A quality of loss
    Affecting our content,
As trade had suddenly encroached
    Upon a sacrament.

EMILY DICKINSON

SLOW SPRING

O year, grow slowly. Exquisite, holy,
    The days go on
With almonds showing the pink stars blowing,
    And birds in the dawn.

Grow slowly, year, like a child that is dear,
    Or a lamb that is mild,
By little steps, and by little skips,
    Like a lamb or a child.

KATHARINE TYNAN

SPRING QUIET

Gone were but the Winter,
    Come were but the Spring,
I would go to a covert
    Where the birds sing;

Where in the whitethorn
    Singeth a thrush,
And a robin sings
    In the holly-bush.

Full of fresh scents
    Are the budding boughs
Arching high over
    A cool green house:

Full of sweet scents,
    And whispering air

Which sayeth softly:
    'We spread no snare;

'Here dwell in safety,
    Here dwell alone,
With a clear stream
    And a mossy stone.

'Here the sun shineth
    Most shadily;
Here is heard an echo
    Of the far sea,
        Though far off it be.'

CHRISTINA ROSSETTI

FROM **TO MY SISTER**

It is the first mild day of March:
Each minute sweeter than before,
The redbreast sings from the tall larch
That stands beside our door.

There is a blessing in the air,
Which seems a sense of joy to yield
To the bare trees, and mountains bare,
And grass in the green field.

WILLIAM WORDSWORTH

THE LENT LILY

'Tis spring; come out to ramble
    The hilly brakes around,
For under thorn and bramble
    About the hollow ground
    The primroses are found.

And there's the windflower chilly
    With all the winds at play,
And there's the Lenten lily
    That has not long to stay
    And dies on Easter day.

And since till girls go maying
    You find the primrose still,
And find the windflower playing
    With every wind at will,
    But not the daffodil,

Bring baskets now, and sally
    Upon the spring's array,
And bear from hill and valley
    The daffodil away
    That dies on Easter day.

A. E. HOUSMAN

MARCH

Blossom on the plum,
    Wild wind and merry;
    Leaves on the cherry,
And one swallow come.

Red windy dawn,
    Swift rain and sunny;
    Wild bees seeking honey,
Crocus on the lawn;
    Blossom on the plum.

Grass begins to grow,
    Dandelions come;
Snowdrops haste to go
After last month's snow;
Rough winds beat and blow,
    Blossom on the plum.

NORA HOPPER

SPRING GOETH ALL IN WHITE

Spring goeth all in white,
Crowned with milk-white may[†]:
In fleecy flocks of light
O'er heaven the white clouds stray:

    White butterflies in the air;
White daisies prank the ground:
The cherries and the hoary pear
Scatter their snow around.

    ROBERT BRIDGES

[†] *a spring-flowering shrub*

LOVELIEST OF TREES

Loveliest of trees, the cherry now
Is hung with bloom along the bough,
And stands about the woodland ride
Wearing white for Eastertide.

Now, of my threescore years and ten,
Twenty will not come again,
And take from seventy springs a score,
It only leaves me fifty more.

And since to look at things in bloom
Fifty springs are little room,
About the woodlands I will go
To see the cherry hung with snow.

    A. E. HOUSMAN

SONG ON MAY MORNING

Now the bright morning star, Day's harbinger,
Comes dancing from the east, and leads with her
The flowery May, who from her green lap throws
The yellow cowslip and the pale primrose.
      Hail, bounteous May, that dost inspire
      Mirth, and youth, and warm desire!
      Woods and groves are of thy dressing;
      Hill and dale doth boast thy blessing.
Thus we salute thee with our early song,
And welcome thee, and wish thee long.

JOHN MILTON

SPRING

Nothing is so beautiful as spring—
      When weeds, in wheels, shoot long and lovely and lush;
      Thrush's eggs look little low heavens, and thrush
Through the echoing timber does so rinse and wring
The ear, it strikes like lightnings to hear him sing;
      The glassy peartree leaves and blooms, they brush
      The descending blue; that blue is all in a rush
With richness; the racing lambs too have fair their fling.

What is all this juice and all this joy?
      A strain of the earth's sweet being in the beginning
In Eden garden.— Have, get, before it cloy,
      Before it cloud, Christ, lord, and sour with sinning,
Innocent mind and Mayday in girl and boy,
      Most, O Maid's child, thy choice and worthy the winning.

GERARD MANLEY HOPKINS

SONNET

From you I have been absent in the spring,
When proud-pied April, dress'd in all his trim,
Hath put a spirit of youth in everything,
That heavy Saturn laugh'd and leap'd with him.
Yet nor the lays of birds, nor the sweet smell
Of different flowers in odour and in hue,
Could make me any summer's story tell,
Or from their proud lap pluck them where they grew;
Nor did I wonder at the Lily's white
Nor praise the deep vermilion in the Rose;
They were but sweet, but figures of delight,
Drawn after you, you pattern of all those.
    Yet seem'd it Winter still, and you away,
    As with your shadow I with these did play.

WILLIAM SHAKESPEARE

FROM **TO A NIGHTINGALE**

I cannot see what flowers are at my feet,
    Nor what soft incense hangs upon the boughs,
But, in embalmed darkness, guess each sweet
    Wherewith the seasonable month endows
The grass, the thicket, and the fruit-tree wild;
    White hawthorn, and the pastoral eglantine;
      Fast-fading violets cover'd up in leaves;
      And mid-May's eldest child,
    The coming musk-rose, full of dewy wine,
      The murmurous haunt of flies on summer eves.

JOHN KEATS

THE QUESTION

I dream'd that, as I wander'd by the way,
    Bare Winter suddenly was turned to Spring;
And gentle odours led my steps astray,
    Mix'd with a sound of waters murmuring
Along a shelving bank of turf, which lay
    Under a copse, and hardly dared to fling
Its green arms round the bosom of the stream,
But kiss'd it and then fled, as thou mightest in dream.

There grew pied wind-flowers and violets;
    Daisies, those pearl'd Arcturi of the earth,
The constellated flower that never sets;
    Faint oxlips; tender bluebells, at whose birth
The sod scarce heaved; and that tall flower that wets—
    Like a child, half in tenderness and mirth—
Its mother's face with heaven-collected tears
When the low wind, its playmate's voice, it hears.

And in the warm hedge grew lush eglantine,
    Green cowbind and the moonlight-colour'd May[†]:
And cherry-blossoms, and white cups whose wine
    Was the bright dew yet drain'd not by the day;
And wild roses, and ivy serpentine,
    With its dark buds and leaves wandering astray;
And flowers, azure, black, and streak'd with gold,
Fairer than any waken'd eyes behold.

And nearer to the river's trembling edge
    There grew broad flag-flowers, purple prank'd with white,

†*a spring-flowering shrub*

And starry river-buds among the sedge,
    And floating water-lilies, broad and bright,
Which lit the oak that overhung the hedge
    With moonlight beams of their own watery light;
And bulrushes, and reeds of such deep green
As soothed the dazzled eye with sober sheen.

Methought that of those visionary flowers
    I made a nosegay, bound in such a way
That the same hues which in their natural bowers
    Were mingled or opposed, the like array
Kept these imprison'd children of the Hours
    Within my hand;—and then, elate and gay,
I hasten'd to the spot whence I had come,
That I might there present it—O! to whom?

PERCY BYSSHE SHELLEY

FROM **INTIMATIONS OF IMMORTALITY**

> Land and sea
> Give themselves up to jollity,
> And with the heart of May
> Doth every beast keep holiday;—
> Thou Child of Joy,
> Shout round me, let me hear thy shouts, thou happy Shepherd-boy!

* * * * *

> Oh evil day! if I were sullen
> While Earth herself is adorning
> This sweet May-morning,
> And the children are culling
> On every side
> In a thousand valleys far and wide,
> Fresh flowers; while the sun shines warm,
> And the Babe leaps up on his Mother's arm:—
> I hear, I hear, with joy I hear!

* * * * *

> Then sing, ye Birds, sing, sing a joyous song!
> And let the young lambs bound
> As to the tabor's sound!
> We in thought will join your throng,
> Ye that pipe and ye that play,
> Ye that through your hearts today
> Feel the gladness of the May!

WILLIAM WORDSWORTH

COMPOSED ON
A MAY MORNING, 1838

Life with yon Lambs, like day, is just begun,
Yet Nature seems to them a heavenly guide.
Does joy approach? they meet the coming tide;
And sullenness avoid, as now they shun
Pale twilight's lingering glooms,—and in the sun
Couch near their dams, with quiet satisfied;
Or gambol—each with his shadow at his side,
Varying its shape wherever he may run.
As they from turf yet hoar with sleepy dew
All turn, and court the shining and the green,
Where herbs look up, and opening flowers are seen;
Why to God's goodness cannot we be true,
And so, His gifts and promises between,
Feed to the last on pleasures ever new?

WILLIAM WORDSWORTH

May is lilac here in New England,
May is a thrush singing 'Sun up!' on a tip-top ash-tree,
May is white clouds behind pine-trees
Puffed out and marching upon a blue sky.
May is a green as no other,
May is much sun through small leaves,
May is soft earth,
And apple-blossoms,
And windows open to a South wind.
May is a full light wind of lilac
From Canada to Narragansett Bay.

                    AMY LOWELL

EVERYONE SANG

Everyone suddenly burst out singing;
And I was filled with such delight
As prisoned birds must find in freedom
Winging wildly across the white
Orchards and dark-green fields; on; on; and out of sight.

Everyone's voice was suddenly lifted,
And beauty came like the setting sun.
My heart was shaken with tears; and horror
Drifted away . . . O but every one
Was a bird; and the song was wordless; the singing
      will never be done.

            SIEGFRIED SASSOON

A MEMORY

Four ducks on a pond,
A grass-bank beyond,
A blue sky of spring,
White clouds on the wing:
What a little thing
To remember for years—
To remember with tears!

        WILLIAM ALLINGHAM

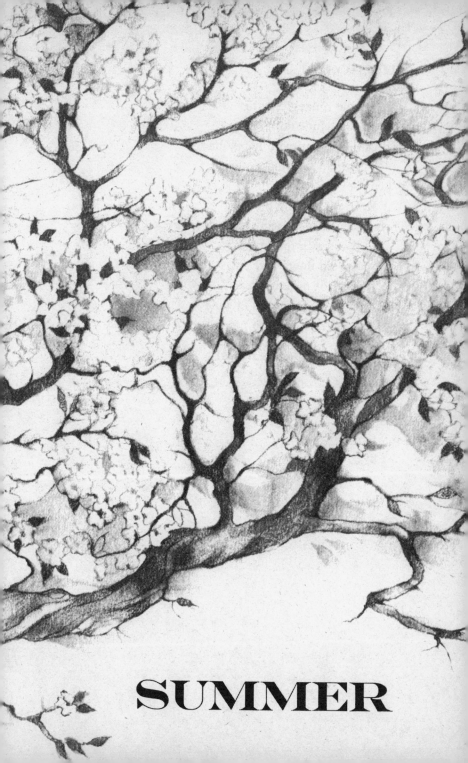

SUMMER

THE ROSE

Whenas the mildest month
    Of jolly June doth spring,
And gardens green with happy hue
    Their famous fruits do bring;
When eke[†] the lustiest time
    Reviveth youthly blood,
Then springs the finest featured flower
    In border fair that stood.
Which moveth me to say,
    In time of pleasant year,
Of all the pleasant flowers in June
    The red rose hath no peer.

THOMAS HOWELL

[†]*also*

FROM THE VISION OF SIR LAUNFAL

And what is so rare as a day in June?
    Then, if ever, come perfect days;
Then Heaven tries earth if it be in tune,
    And over it softly her warm ear lays;
Whether we look, or whether we listen,
We hear life murmur, or see it glisten;
Every clod feels a stir of might,
    An instinct within it that reaches and towers,
And groping blindly above it for light,
    Climbs to a soul in grass and flowers;
The flush of life may well be seen
    Thrilling back over hills and valleys;
The cowslip startles in meadows green,
    The buttercup catches the sun in its chalice,
And there's never a leaf or blade too mean
    To be some happy creature's palace;
The little bird sits at his door in the sun,
    Atilt like a blossom among the leaves,
And lets his illumined being o'errun
    With the deluge of summer it receives;
His mate feels the eggs beneath her wings,
And the heart in her dumb breast flutters and sings;
He sings to the wide world, and she to her nest,—
In the nice ear of Nature which song is the best?

JAMES RUSSELL LOWELL

PRELUDE

Pleasant it was, when woods were green,
    And winds were soft and low,
To lie amid some sylvan scene,
Where, the long drooping boughs between,
Shadows dark and sunlight sheen
    Alternate come and go.

Or where the denser grove receives
    No sunlight from above,
But the dark foliage interweaves
In one unbroken roof of leaves,
Underneath whose sloping eaves
    The shadows hardly move.

Beneath some patriarchal tree
    I lay upon the ground;
His hoary arms uplifted he,
And all the broad leaves over me
Clapped their little hands in glee,
    With one continuous sound;—

A slumberous sound—a sound that brings
    The feelings of a dream,—
As of innumerable wings,
As, when a bell no longer swings,
Faint the hollow murmur rings
    O'er meadow, lake, and stream.

And dreams of that which cannot die,
    Bright visions, came to me,

As lapped in thought I used to lie,
And gaze into the summer sky,
Where the sailing clouds went by,
	Like ships upon the sea.

HENRY WADSWORTH LONGFELLOW

FROM **SLEEP AND POETRY**

What is more gentle than a wind in summer?
What is more soothing than the pretty hummer
That stays one moment in an open flower,
And buzzes cheerfully from bower to bower?
What is more tranquil than a musk-rose blowing
In a green island, far from all men's knowing?

       *   *   *   *   *

What, but thee, Sleep? Soft closer of our eyes!
Low murmurer of tender lullabies!
Light hoverer around our happy pillows!
Wreather of poppy buds, and weeping willows!
Silent entangler of a beauty's tresses!
Most happy listener! when the morning blesses
Thee for enlivening all the cheerful eyes
That glance so brightly at the new sun-rise.

JOHN KEATS

I stood tiptoe upon a little hill,
The air was cooling, and so very still,
That the sweet buds which with a modest pride
Pull droopingly, in slanting curve aside,
Their scanty-leaved, and fine tapering stems,
Had not yet lost their starry diadems
Caught from the early sobbing of the morn.
The clouds were pure and white as flocks new-shorn,
And fresh from the clear brook; sweetly they slept
On the blue fields of heaven, and then there crept
A little noiseless noise among the leaves,
Born of the very sigh that silence heaves;
For not the faintest motion could be seen
Of all the shades that slanted o'er the green.
There was wide wandering for the greediest eye,
To peer about upon variety;
Far round the horizon's crystal air to skim,
And trace the dwindled edgings of its brim;
To picture out the quaint and curious bending
Of a fresh woodland alley never ending:
Or by the bowery clefts, and leafy shelves,
Guess where the jaunty streams refresh themselves.
I gazed awhile, and felt as light and free
As though the fanning wings of Mercury
Had play'd upon my heels: I was light-hearted,
And many pleasures to my vision started;
So I straightway began to pluck a posy
Of luxuries bright, milky, soft, and rosy.
A bush of May-flowers with the bees about them;

Ah, sure no tasteful nook could be without them!
And let a lush laburnum oversweep them,
And let long grass grow round the roots, to keep them
Moist, cool, and green; and shade the violets,
That they may bind the moss in leafy nets.

A filbert hedge with wildbriar overtwined,
And clumps of woodbine taking the soft wind
Upon their summer thrones; there too should be
The frequent chequer of a youngling tree,
That with a score of light green brethren shoots
From the quaint mossiness of aged roots:
Round which is heard a spring-head of clear waters,
Babbling so wildly of its lovely daughters,
The spreading bluebells: it may haply mourn
That such fair clusters should be rudely torn
From their fresh beds, and scattered thoughtlessly
By infant hands, left on the path to die.

*　*　*　*　*

Here are sweet peas, on tiptoe for a flight
With wings of gentle flush o'er delicate white
And taper fingers catching at all things,
To bind them all about with tiny rings.
Linger awhile upon some bending planks
That lean against a streamlet's rushy banks,
And watch intently Nature's gentle doings:
They will be found softer than ringdoves' cooings.
How silent comes the water round that bend!
Not the minutest whisper does it send

To the o'erhanging sallows†: blades of grass
Slowly across the chequered shadows pass.
Why, you might read two sonnets, ere they reach
To where the hurrying freshnesses aye preach
A natural sermon o'er their pebbly beds;
Where swarms of minnows show their little heads,
Staying their wavy bodies 'gainst the streams,
To taste the luxury of sunny beams
Temper'd with coolness. How they ever wrestle
With their own sweet delight, and ever nestle
Their silver bellies on the pebbly sand!
If you but scantily hold out the hand,
That very instant not one will remain;
But turn your eye, and they are there again.
The ripples seem right glad to reach those cresses,
And cool themselves among the emerald tresses;
The while they cool themselves, they freshness give,
And moisture, that the bowery green may live:
So keeping up an interchange of favours,
Like good men in the truth of their behaviours.
Sometimes goldfinches one by one will drop
From low-hung branches: little space they stop
But sip, and twitter, and their feathers sleek;
Then off at once, as in a wanton freak:
Or perhaps, to show their black and golden wings,
Pausing upon their yellow flutterings.

JOHN KEATS

†*willows*

SUMMER

Winter is cold-hearted,
    Spring is yea and nay,
Autumn is a weathercock
    Blown every way:
Summer days for me
When every leaf is on its tree;

When Robin's not a beggar,
    And Jenny Wren's a bride,
And larks hang singing, singing, singing,
    Over the wheat-fields wide,
    And anchored lilies ride,
And the pendulum spider
    Swings from side to side,

And blue-black beetles transact business,
    And gnats fly in a host,
And furry caterpillars hasten
    That no time be lost,
And moths grow fat and thrive,
And ladybirds arrive.

Before green apples blush,
    Before green nuts embrown,
Why, one day in the country
    Is worth a month in town;
    Is worth a day and a year
Of the dusty, musty, lag-last fashion
    That days drone elsewhere.

CHRISTINA ROSSETTI

FROM THYRSIS

So, some tempestuous morn in early June,
   When the year's primal burst of bloom is o'er
      Before the roses and the longest day—
When garden-walks, and all the grassy floor,
     With blossoms, red and white, of fallen May[†],
      And chestnut flowers are strewn—
So have I heard the cuckoo's parting cry,
   From the wet field, through the vext garden-trees,
   Come with the volleying rain and tossing breeze:
The bloom is gone and with the bloom go I.

Too quick despairer, wherefore wilt thou go?
   Soon will the high Midsummer pomps come on,
     Soon will the musk carnations break and swell,
Soon shall we have gold-dusted snapdragon,
     Sweet William with its homely cottage-smell,
      And stocks in fragrant blow;
Roses that down the alleys shine afar,
   And open, jasmine-muffled lattices,
   And groups under the dreaming garden trees,
And the full moon, and the white evening-star.

MATTHEW ARNOLD

ON THE GRASSHOPPER
AND CRICKET

The poetry of earth is never dead:
    When all the birds are faint with the hot sun,
    And hide in cooling trees, a voice will run
From hedge to hedge about the new-mown mead.
That is the grasshopper's—he takes the lead
    In summer luxury,—he has never done
    With his delights, for when tired out with fun,
He rests at ease beneath some pleasant weed.
The poetry of earth is ceasing never;
    On a long winter evening, when the frost
Has wrought a silence, from the stove there shrills
The Cricket's song, in warmth increasing ever,
    And seems to one in drowsiness half lost,
The Grasshopper's among some grassy hills.

JOHN KEATS

Loud is the summer's busy song,
The smallest breeze can find a tongue,
While insects of each tiny size
Grow teazing with their melodies,
Till noon burns with its blistering breath
Around, and day lies still as death.
The busy noise of man and brute
Is on a sudden lost and mute;
Even the brook that leaps along
Seems weary of its bubbling song,
And, so soft its waters creep,
Tired silence sinks in sounder sleep.
The cricket on its banks is dumb,
The very flies forget to hum;
And, save the waggon rocking round,
The landscape sleeps without a sound.
The breeze is stopt, the lazy bough
Hath not a leaf that dances now;
The tottergrass upon the hill,
And spiders' threads, are standing still;
The feathers dropt from moorhen's wing,
Which to the water's surface cling,
Are steadfast, and as heavy seem
As stones beneath them in the stream;
Hawkweed and groundsel's fanning downs
Unruffled keep their seedy crowns;
And in the oven-heated air,
Not one light thing is floating there,
Save that to the earnest eye,
The restless heat seems twittering by.

Noon swoons beneath the heat it made,
And flowers e'en wither in the shade,
Until the sun slopes in the west,
Like weary traveller, glad to rest,
On pillowed clouds of many hues;
Then nature's voice its joy renews,
And chequer'd field and grassy plain
Hum, with their summer songs again,
A requiem to the day's decline,
Whose setting sunbeams coolly shine,
As welcome to day's feeble powers
As falling dews to thirsty flowers.

JOHN CLARE

AMENDS TO NATURE

I have loved colours, and not flowers;
Their motion, not the swallow's wings;
And wasted more than half my hours
Without the comradeship of things.

How is it, now, that I can see,
With love and wonder and delight,
The children of the hedge and tree,
The little lords of day and night?

How is it that I see the roads,
No longer with usurping eyes,
A twilight meeting-place for toads,
A mid-day mart for butterflies?

I feel, in every midge that hums,
Life, fugitive and infinite,
And suddenly the world becomes
A part of me and I of it.

ARTHUR SYMONS

RAIN IN SUMMER

How beautiful is the rain!
After the dust and heat,
In the broad and fiery street,
In the narrow lane,
How beautiful is the rain!

How it clatters along the roofs,
Like the tramp of hoofs!
How it gushes and struggles out
From the throat of the overflowing spout!
Across the window-pane
It pours and pours;
And swift and wide,
With a muddy tide,
Like a river down the gutter roars
The rain, the welcome rain!

* * * * *

In the country, on every side,
Where far and wide,
Like a leopard's tawny and spotted hide,
Stretches the plain,
To the dry grass and drier grain
How welcome is the rain!

In the furrowed land
The toilsome and patient oxen stand;
Lifting the yoke-encumbered head,
With their dilated nostrils spread,
They silently inhale
The clover-scented gale,

And the vapors that arise
From the well-watered and smoking soil.
For this rest in the furrow after toil
Their large and lustrous eyes
Seem to thank the Lord,
More than man's spoken word.

Near at hand,
From under the sheltering trees,
The farmer sees
His pastures, and his fields of grain,
As they bend their tops
To the numberless beating drops
Of the incessant rain.
He counts it as no sin
That he sees therein
Only his own thrift and gain.

These, and far more than these,
The Poet sees!
He can behold
Aquarius old
Walking the fenceless fields of air;
And from each ample fold
Of the clouds about him rolled
Scattering everywhere
The showery rain,
As the farmer scatters his grain.

He can behold
Things manifold
That have not yet been wholly told,—
Have not been wholly sung nor said.

For his thought, that never stops,
Follows the water-drops
Down to the graves of the dead,
Down through chasms and gulfs profound,
To the dreary fountain-head
Of lakes and rivers under ground;
And sees them, when the rain is done,
On the bridge of colors seven
Climbing up once more to heaven,
Opposite the setting sun.

Thus the Seer,
With vision clear,
Sees forms appear and disappear,
In the perpetual round of strange,
Mysterious change
From birth to death, from death to birth,
From earth to heaven, from heaven to earth;
Till glimpses more sublime
Of things unseen before,
Unto his wondering eyes reveal
The Universe, as an immeasurable wheel
Turning forevermore
In the rapid and rushing river of Time.

HENRY WADSWORTH LONGFELLOW

THE HUMBLE-BEE

Burly, dozing humble-bee,
Where thou art is clime for me.
Let them sail for Porto Rique,
Far-off heats through seas to seek;
I will follow thee alone,
Thou animated torrid-zone!
Zigzag steerer, desert cheerer,
Let me chase thy waving lines;
Keep me nearer, me thy hearer,
Singing over shrubs and vines.

Insect lover of the sun,
Joy of thy dominion!
Sailor of the atmosphere;
Swimmer through the waves of air;
Voyager of light and noon;
Epicurean of June;
Wait, I prithee, till I come
Within earshot of thy hum,—
All without is martyrdom.

When the south wind, in May days,
With a net of shining haze
Silvers the horizon wall,
And with softness touching all,
Tints the human countenance
With a color of romance,
And infusing subtle heats,
Turns the sod to violets,
Thou, in sunny solitudes,

Rover of the underwoods,
The green silence dost displace
With thy mellow, breezy bass.

Hot midsummer's petted crone,
Sweet to me thy drowsy tone
Tells of countless sunny hours,
Long days, and solid banks of flowers;
Of gulfs of sweetness without bound
In Indian wildernesses found;
Of Syrian peace, immortal leisure,
Firmest cheer, and bird-like pleasure.

Aught unsavory or unclean
Hath my insect never seen;
But violets and bilberry bells,
Maple-sap and daffodels,
Grass with green flag half-mast high,
Succory to match the sky,
Columbine with horn of honey,
Scented fern and agrimony,
Clover, catchfly, adder's-tongue
And brier-roses, dwelt among;
All beside was unknown waste,
All was picture as he passed.

Wiser far than human seer,
Yellow-breeched philosopher!
Seeing only what is fair,
Sipping only what is sweet,

Thou dost mock at fate and care,
Leave the chaff and take the wheat.
When the fierce northwestern blast
Cools sea and land so far and fast,
Thou already slumberest deep;
Woe and want thou canst outsleep;
Want and woe, which torture us,
Thy sleep makes ridiculous.

RALPH WALDO EMERSON

BALLADE
MADE IN THE HOT WEATHER

Fountains that frisk and sprinkle
The moss they overspill;
Pools that the breezes crinkle;
The wheel beside the mill,
With its wet, weedy frill;
Wind shadows in the wheat;
A water-cart in the street;
The fringe of foam that girds
An island's ferneries;
A green sky's minor thirds—
To live, I think of these!

Of ice and glass the tinkle,
Pellucid, silver-shrill;
Peaches without a wrinkle;
Cherries and snow at will,
From china bowls that fill

The senses with a sweet
Incuriousness of heat;
A melon's dripping sherds†;
Cream-clotted strawberries;
Dusk dairies set with curds—
To live, I think of these!

Vale-lily and periwinkle;
Wet stone-crop on the sill;
The look of leaves a-twinkle
With windlets clear and still;
The feel of a forest rill
That wimples fresh and fleet
About one's naked feet;
The muzzles of drinking herds;
Lush flags and bulrushes;
The chirp of rain-bound birds—
To live, I think of these!

ENVOY

Dark aisles, new packs of cards,
Mermaiden's tails, cool swards,
Dawn dews and starlit seas,
White marbles, whiter words—
To live, I think of these!

WILLIAM ERNEST HENLEY

†*pieces*

AUGUST WEATHER

Dead heat and windless air,
    And silence over all;
Never a leaf astir,
    But the ripe apples fall;
Plums are purple red,
    Pears amber and brown;
Thud! in the garden-bed!
    Ripe apples fall down.

Air like a cider press
    With the bruised apples' scent;
Low whistles express
    Some sleepy bird's content;
Still world and windless sky,
    A mist of heat o'er all;
Peace like a lullaby,
    And the ripe apples fall.

KATHARINE TYNAN

SILENCE

It was bright day and all the trees were still
In the deep valley, and the dim Sun glowed;
The clay in hard-baked fire along the hill
Leapt through dark trunks to apples green and gold,
Smooth, hard and cold, they shone like lumps of stone.

They were bright bubbles bursting from the trees,
Swollen and still among the dark green boughs;
On their bright skins the shadows of the leaves
Seemed the faint ghosts of summers long since gone,
Faint ghosts of ghosts, the dreams of ghostly eyes.

There was no sound between those breathless hills.
Only the dim Sun hung there, nothing moved;
The thronged, massed, crowded multitude of leaves
Hung like dumb tongues that loll and gasp for air:
The grass was thick and still, between the trees.

There were big apples lying on the ground,
Shining, quite still, as though they had been stunned
By some great violent spirit stalking through,
Leaving a deep and supernatural calm
Round a dead beetle upturned in a furrow.

A valley filled with dark, quiet, leaf-thick trees,
Loaded with green, cold, faintly shining suns;
And in the sky a great dim burning disc!—
Madness it is to watch these twisted trunks
And to see nothing move and hear no sound!

Let's make a noise, Hey! . . . Hey! . . . Hullo! Hullo!

W. J. TURNER

THE NIGHT-WIND

In summer's mellow midnight,
A cloudless moon shone through
Our open parlor window
And rose-trees wet with dew.

I sat in silent musing,
The soft wind waved my hair:
It told me Heaven was glorious,
And sleeping earth was fair.

I needed not its breathing
To bring such thoughts to me,
But still it whispered lowly,
'How dark the woods will be!

'The thick leaves in my murmur
Are rustling like a dream,
And all their myriad voices
Instinct with spirit seem.'

I said, 'Go, gentle singer,
Thy wooing voice is kind,
But do not think its music
Has power to reach my mind.

'Play with the scented flower,
The young tree's supple bough,
And leave my human feelings
In their own course to flow.'

The wanderer would not leave me;
Its kiss grew warmer still—

'O come,' it sighed so sweetly,
'I'll win thee 'gainst thy will.

'Have we not been from childhood friends?
Have I not loved thee long?
As long as thou hast loved the night
Whose silence wakes my song.

'And when thy heart is laid at rest
Beneath the churchyard stone
I shall have time enough to mourn
And thou to be alone.'

                    EMILY BRONTË

DOG-DAYS

A ladder sticking up at the open window,
The top of an old ladder;
And all of Summer is there.

Great waves and tufts of wistaria surge across the window,
And a thin, belated blossom
Jerks up and down in the sunlight;
Purple translucence against the blue sky.
"Tie back this branch," I say,
But my hands are sticky with leaves,
And my nostrils widen to the smell of crushed green.
The ladder moves uneasily at the open window,
And I call to the man beneath,
"Tie back that branch."

There is a ladder leaning against the window-sill,
And a mutter of thunder in the air.

AMY LOWELL

THE SECRET

A secret is a secret, any size.
Sometimes it may be filling for good pies,
Powdered blue, and coming in small spheres,
Where every now and then a fire clears
The balsams from a hillside, strips it clean,
And seeds nobody plants send up their green,
The hairy little fists that will be brake
And spikes of bells that smell like new-made cake,

And feel like cake to touch, and mullein candles
With leaves a man finds woolen when he handles.

Two Summers of oven heat, and there you are!
You are up, along with the morning star,
So neighbors will not see your telltale pail.
Through the birches, over the pasture rail—
Perhaps you leave a piece of you just there
To show the birds what color pants you wear.
You sink in dewy bushes on all fours.
The spiders sit imprisoned at the cores
Of necklaces on diamonds, string on string.
They cannot move for the night's jewelling.
The sun is huge between the granite ledges,
The blueberry leaves have diamonds on their edges.
The berries drum your pail. The morning sky
Shuts down blue around you. On your thigh
An inchworm humps and stretches, comes to where
He can only feel the empty air
And wave his head about. In woods below
A dozen oven-birds begin to go.
Suddenly before your very nose
A brazen, spotted freckle-lily grows,
Quivering with color to the core;
It was not there the instant just before;
And now your eyes are used to such bright red,
You notice all of twenty just ahead.
You would not be so bold to look at these
If your pants were still above your knees
And you had a boy's nose on your face
To catch a batch of freckles from their lace.
The blueberries hang in clusters from the green

Without an underdone one in between,
You get a handful from a single pull.
You grow clumsy as your pail gets full.
Your fingers now are getting to be thumbs,
You listen to each bumble-bee that hums.
Locusts tune their fiddle-strings up taut,
It's clear it's going to be ungodly hot.
The pail fills slowest when it's near the top.
The sun has got inside you, and you stop.

You go home slowly, but keep to the woods,
So nobody around will see your goods.
There's no sense letting everybody know
Where the biggest blueberries this year grow,
And you may want to have a pie or two
Tomorrow, and you wouldn't if folks knew.

ROBERT P. TRISTRAM COFFIN

THE RUSTLING OF GRASS

I cannot tell why,
But the rustling of grass,
As the summer winds pass
Through the field where I lie,
Bring to life a lost day,
Long ago, far away,
When in childhood I lay
Looking up at the sky
And the white clouds that pass,
Trailing isles of grey shadow
Across the gold grass . . .

O, the dreams that drift by
With the slow flowing years,
Hopes, Memories, tears,
In the rustling grass.

ALFRED NOYES

FERN HILL

Now as I was young and easy under the apple boughs
About the lilting house and happy as the grass was green,
    The night above the dingle starry,
      Time let me hail and climb
     Golden in the heydays of his eyes,
And honoured among wagons I was prince of the apple towns
And once below a time I lordly had the trees and leaves
      Trail with daisies and barley
     Down the rivers of the windfall light.

And as I was green and carefree, famous among the barns
About the happy yard and singing as the farm was home,
     In the sun that is young once only,
      Time let me play and be
     Golden on the mercy of his means,
And green and golden I was huntsman and herdsman, the calves
Sang to my horn, the foxes on the hill barked clear and cold,
      And the sabbath rang slowly
     In the pebbles of the holy streams.

All the sun long it was running, it was lovely, the hay
Fields high as the house, the tunes from the chimneys, it was air
     And playing, lovely and watery
      And fire green as grass.
     And nightly under the simple stars
As I rode to sleep the owls were bearing the farm away,
All the moon long I heard, blessed among stables, the nightjars
      Flying with the ricks, and the horses
       Flashing into the dark.

And then to awake, and the farm, like a wanderer white

With the dew, come back, the cock on his shoulder: it was all
    Shining, it was Adam and maiden,
      The sky gathered again
    And the sun grew round that very day.
So it must have been after the birth of the simple light
In the first, spinning place, the spellbound horses walking warm
    Out of the whinnying green stable
      On to the fields of praise.

And honoured among foxes and pheasants by the gay house
Under the newmade clouds and happy as the heart was long
    In the sun born over and over,
      I ran my heedless ways,
    My wishes raced through the house high hay
And nothing I cared, at my sky blue trades, that time allows
In all his tuneful turning so few and such morning songs
    Before the children green and golden
      Follow him out of grace.

Nothing I cared, in the lamb white days, that time would take me
Up to the swallow thronged loft by the shadow of my hand,
    In the moon that is always rising,
      Nor that riding to sleep
    I should hear him fly with the high fields
And wake to the farm forever fled from the childless land.
Oh, as I was young and easy in the mercy of his means,
    Time held me green and dying
    Though I sang in my chains like the sea.

DYLAN THOMAS

HEAT

O wind, rend open the heat,
Cut apart the heat,
Rend it to tatters.

Fruit cannot drop
Through this thick air—
Fruit cannot fall into heat
That presses up and blunts
The points of pears
And rounds the grapes.

Cut the heat—
Plough through it,
Turning it on either side
Of your path.

H. D.

THE RAIN

I hear leaves drinking rain;
    I hear rich leaves on top
Giving the poor beneath
    Drop after drop;
'Tis a sweet noise to hear
These green leaves drinking near.

And when the Sun comes out,
    After this rain shall stop,

A wondrous light will fill
  Each dark, round drop;
I hope the Sun shines bright;
'Twill be a lovely sight.

W. H. DAVIES

WILD STRAWBERRIES

Strawberries that in gardens grow
  Are plump and juicy fine,
But sweeter far, as wise men know,
  Spring from the woodland vine.

No need for bowl or silver spoon,
  Sugar or spice or cream,
Has the wild berry plucked in June
  Beside the trickling stream.

One such, to melt at the tongue's root
  Confounding taste with scent,
Beats a full peck of garden fruit:
  Which points my argument:—

May sudden justice overtake
  And snap the froward pen,
That old and palsied poets shake
  Against the minds of men.

Blasphemers trusting to hold caught
  In far-flung webs of ink
The utmost ends of human thought
  Till nothing's left to think.

But may the gift of heavenly peace
    And glory for all time
Keep the boy Tom who tending geese
    First made the nursery rhyme.

ROBERT GRAVES

THESE ARE THE DAYS
WHEN BIRDS COME BACK

These are the days when birds come back,
A very few, a bird or two,
To take a backward look.

These are the days when skies put on
The old, old sophistries of June,—
A blue and gold mistake.

Oh, fraud that cannot cheat the bee,
Almost thy plausibility
Induces my belief,

Till ranks of seed their witness bear,
And softly through the altered air
Hurries a timid leaf!

Oh, sacrament of summer days,
Oh, last communion in the haze,
Permit a child to join,

Thy sacred emblems to partake,
Thy consecrated bread to break,
Taste thine immortal wine!

EMILY DICKINSON

AS IMPERCEPTIBLY AS GRIEF

As imperceptibly as grief
The summer lapsed away,—
Too imperceptible, at last,
To seem like perfidy.

A quietness distilled,
As twilight long begun,
Or Nature, spending with herself
Sequestered afternoon.

The dusk drew earlier in,
The morning foreign shone,—
A courteous, yet harrowing grace,
As guest who would be gone.

And thus, without a wing,
Or service of a keel,
Our summer made her light escape
Into the beautiful.

EMILY DICKINSON

AUTUMN

TO AUTUMN

Season of mists and mellow fruitfulness!
    Close bosom friend of the maturing sun;
Conspiring with him how to load and bless
    With fruit the vines that round the thatch-eaves run;
To bend with apples the moss'd cottage-trees,
    And fill all fruit with ripeness to the core;
      To swell the gourd, and plump the hazel shells
    With a sweet kernel; to set budding more,
And still more, later flowers for the bees,
Until they think warm days will never cease,
      For summer has o'erbrimmed their clammy cells.

Who hath not seen thee oft amid thy store?
    Sometimes whoever seeks abroad may find
Thee sitting careless on a granary floor,
    Thy hair soft-lifted by the winnowing wind;
Or on a half-reap'd furrow sound asleep,
    Drowsed with the fumes of poppies, while thy hook
      Spares the next swath and all its twined flowers;
And sometimes like a gleaner thou dost keep
    Steady thy laden head across a brook,
    Or by a cider-press, with patient look,
      Thou watchest the last oozings, hours by hours.

Where are the songs of spring? Ay, where are they?
    Think not of them, thou hast thy music too,
While barred clouds bloom the soft-dying day,
    And touch the stubble-plains with rosy hue;
Then in a wailful choir, the small gnats mourn
    Among the river sallows[†], borne aloft
      Or sinking as the light wind lives or dies;

[†]willows

94

And full-grown lambs loud bleat from hilly bourn;
Hedge-crickets sing, and now with treble soft
The redbreast whistles from a garden croft,
And gathering swallows twitter in the skies.

JOHN KEATS

RICH DAYS

Welcome to you rich Autumn days,
Ere comes the cold, leaf-picking wind;
When golden stooks† are seen in fields,
All standing arm-in-arm entwined;
And gallons of sweet cider seen
On trees in apples red and green.

With mellow pears that cheat our teeth,
Which melt that tongues may suck them in;
With cherries red, and blue-black plums,
Now sweet and soft from stone to skin;
And woodnuts rich, to make us go
Into the loneliest lanes we know.

W. H. DAVIES

†*shocks*

ODE—AUTUMN

I saw old Autumn in the misty morn
Stand shadowless like Silence, listening
To silence, for no lonely bird would sing
Into his hollow ear from woods forlorn,
Nor lowly hedge nor solitary thorn;
Shaking his languid locks all dewy bright,
With tangled gossamer that fell by night,
    Pearling his coronet of golden corn.

Where are the songs of Summer?—With the sun,
Oping the dusky eyelids of the south,
Till shade and silence waken up as one,
And Morning sings with a warm odorous mouth.
Where are the merry birds?—Away, away,
On panting wings through the inclement skies,
    Lest owls should prey
    Undazzled at noon-day,
And tear with horny beak their lustrous eyes.

Where are the blooms of Summer?—In the west,
Blushing their last to the last sunny hours,
When the mild Eve by sudden Night is prest
Like tearful Proserpine, snatch'd from her flow'rs
    To a most gloomy breast.
Where is the pride of Summer,—the green prime,—
The many, many leaves all twinkling?—Three
On the moss'd elm; three on the naked lime
Trembling,—and one upon the old oak tree!
    Where is the Dryad's immortality?—
Gone into mournful cypress and dark yew,

Or wearing the long gloomy Winter through
    In the smooth holly's green eternity.

The squirrel gloats o'er his accomplished hoard,
The ants have brimmed their garners with ripe grain,
    And honey bees have stored
The sweets of summer in their luscious cells;
The swallows all have winged across the main;
But here the Autumn melancholy dwells,
    And sighs her tearful spells
Amongst the sunless shadows of the plain.
    Alone, alone,
    Upon a mossy stone,
She sits and reckons up the dead and gone,
With the last leaves for a love-rosary;
Whilst all the wither'd world looks drearily,
Like a dim picture of the drownèd past
In the hush'd mind's mysterious far-away,
Doubtful what ghostly thing will steal the last
Into that distance, grey upon the grey.

O go and sit with her, and be o'ershaded
Under the languid downfall of her hair;
She wears a coronal of flowers faded
Upon her forehead, and a face of care;—
There is enough of wither'd everywhere
To make her bower,—and enough of gloom;
There is enough of sadness to invite,
If only for the rose that died, whose doom
Is Beauty's,—she that with the living bloom

Of conscious cheeks most beautifies the light;
There is enough of sorrowing, and quite
Enough of bitter fruits the earth doth bear,—
Enough of chilly droppings for her bowl;
Enough of fear and shadowy despair,
To frame her cloudy prison for the soul!

THOMAS HOOD

MOONLIT APPLES

At the top of the house the apples are laid in rows,
And the skylight lets the moonlight in, and those
Apples are deep-sea apples of green. There goes
 A cloud on the moon in the autumn night.

A mouse in the wainscot scratches, and scratches, and then
There is no sound at the top of the house of men
Or mice; and the cloud is blown, and the moon again
 Dapples the apples with deep-sea light.

They are lying in rows there, under the gloomy beams;
On the sagging floor; they gather the silver streams
Out of the moon, those moonlit apples of dreams,
 And quiet is the steep stair under.

In the corridors under there is nothing but sleep.
And stiller than ever on orchard boughs they keep
Tryst with the moon, and deep is the silence, deep
 On moon-washed apples of wonder.

JOHN DRINKWATER

ODE TO THE WEST WIND

O wild West Wind, thou breath of Autumn's being,
    Thou from whose unseen presence the leaves dead
Are driven like ghosts from an enchanter fleeing,

    Yellow, and black, and pale, and hectic red,
Pestilence-stricken multitudes! O thou
    Who chariotest to their dark wintry bed

The wingèd seeds, where they lie cold and low,
    Each like a corpse within its grave, until
Thine azure sister of the Spring shall blow

    Her clarion o'er the sleeping earth, and fill
(Driving sweet buds like flocks to feed in air)
    With living hues and odours plain and hill;

Wild Spirit, which art moving everywhere;
Destroyer and preserver; hear, O hear!

Thou on whose stream, 'mid the steep sky's commotion,
    Loose clouds like earth's decaying leaves are shed,
Shook from the tangled boughs of heaven and ocean,

    Angels of rain and lightning! there are spread
On the blue surface of thine airy surge,
    Like the bright hair uplifted from the head

Of some fierce Maenad, even from the dim verge
    Of the horizon to the zenith's height,
The locks of the approaching storm. Thou dirge

    Of the dying year, to which this closing night
Will be the dome of a vast sepulchre,
    Vaulted with all thy congregated might

Of vapours, from whose solid atmosphere
Black rain, and fire, and hail, will burst: O hear!

Thou who didst waken from his summer dreams

The blue Mediterranean, where he lay,
Lull'd by the coil of his crystalline streams,
    Beside a pumice isle in Baiae's bay,
And saw in sleep old palaces and towers
    Quivering within the wave's intenser day,
All overgrown with azure moss and flowers
    So sweet, the sense faints picturing them! Thou
For whose path the Atlantic's level powers
    Cleave themselves into chasms, while far below
The sea-blooms and the oozy woods which wear
    The sapless foliage of the ocean, know
Thy voice, and suddenly grow gray with fear,
And tremble and despoil themselves: O hear!

If I were a dead leaf thou mightest bear;
    If I were a swift cloud to fly with thee;
A wave to pant beneath thy power, and share
    The impulse of thy strength, only less free
Than thou, O uncontrollable! if even
    I were as in my boyhood, and could be
The comrade of thy wanderings over heaven,
    As then, when to outstrip thy skiey speed
Scarce seemed a vision—I would ne'er have striven
    As thus with thee in prayer in my sore need.
O! lift me as a wave, a leaf, a cloud!
    I fall upon the thorns of life! I bleed!
A heavy weight of hours has chain'd and bow'd
One too like thee—tameless, and swift, and proud.

Make me thy lyre, even as the forest is:
    What if my leaves are falling like its own?

The tumult of thy mighty harmonies
        Will take from both a deep autumnal tone,
Sweet though in sadness. Be thou, Spirit fierce,
        My spirit! Be thou me, impetuous one!
Drive my dead thoughts over the universe,
        Like wither'd leaves, to quicken a new birth;
And, by the incantation of this verse,

        Scatter, as from an unextinguished hearth
Ashes and sparks, my words among mankind!
        Be through my lips to unawaken'd earth
The trumpet of a prophecy! O Wind,
If Winter comes, can Spring be far behind?

PERCY BYSSHE SHELLEY

SEPTEMBER

Now every day the bracken browner grows,
        Even the purple stars
        Of clematis, that shone about the bars,
Grow browner; and the little autumn rose
        Dons, for her rosy gown,
        Sad weeds of brown.

Now falls the eve; and ere the morning sun,
        Many a flower her sweet life will have lost,
        Slain by the bitter frost,
Who slays the butterflies also, one by one,
        The tiny beasts
        That go about their business and their feasts.

MARY COLERIDGE

AUTUMN

With what a glory comes and goes the year!
The buds of spring, those beautiful harbingers
Of sunny skies and cloudless times, enjoy
Life's newness, and earth's garniture spread out;
And when the silver habit of the clouds
Comes down upon the autumn sun, and with
A sober gladness the old year takes up
His bright inheritance of golden fruits,
A pomp and pageant fill the splendid scene.

There is a beautiful spirit breathing now
Its mellow richness on the clustered trees,
And, from a beaker full of richest dyes,
Pouring new glory on the autumn woods,
And dipping in warm light the pillared clouds.
Morn on the mountain, like a summer bird,
Lifts up her purple wing, and in the vales
The gentle wind, a sweet and passionate wooer,
Kisses the blushing leaf, and stirs up life
Within the solemn woods of ash deep-crimsoned,
And silver beech, and maple yellow-leafed,
Where Autumn, like a faint old man, sits down
By the wayside a-weary. Through the trees
The golden robin moves. The purple finch,
That on wild cherry and red cedar feeds,
A winter bird, comes with its plaintive whistle,
And pecks by the witch-hazel, whilst aloud
From cottage roofs the warbling bluebird sings,
And merrily, with oft-repeated stroke,
Sounds from the threshing floor the busy flail.

Oh, what a glory doth this world put on
For him who, with a fervent heart, goes forth
Under the bright and glorious sky, and looks
On duties well performed, and days well spent!
For him the wind, ay, and the yellow leaves,
Shall have a voice, and give him eloquent teachings.
He shall so hear the solemn hymn that Death
Has lifted up for all, that he shall go
To his long resting place without a tear.

HENRY WADSWORTH LONGFELLOW

THE MORNS ARE MEEKER
THAN THEY WERE

The morns are meeker than they were,
The nuts are getting brown;
The berry's cheek is plumper,
The rose is out of town.

The maple wears a gayer scarf,
The field a scarlet gown.
Lest I should be old-fashioned,
I'll put a trinket on.

EMILY DICKINSON

TO AUTUMN

O Autumn, laden with fruit, and stained
With the blood of the grape, pass not, but sit
Beneath my shady roof; there thou may'st rest,
And tune thy jolly voice to my fresh pipe;
And all the daughters of the year shall dance!
Sing now the lusty song of fruits and flowers.

"The narrow bud opens her beauties to
"The sun, and love runs in her thrilling veins;
"Blossoms hang round the brows of morning, and
"Flourish down the bright cheek of modest eve,
"Till clust'ring Summer breaks forth into singing,
"And feather'd clouds strew flowers round her head.

"The spirits of the air live on the smells
"Of fruit; and joy, with pinions light, roves round
"The gardens, or sits singing in the trees."
Thus sang the jolly Autumn as he sat;
Then rose, girded himself, and o'er the bleak
Hills fled from our sight; but left his golden load.

WILLIAM BLAKE

FROM **THE GARDEN**

What wondrous life is this I lead!
Ripe apples drop about my head;
The luscious clusters of the vine
Upon my mouth do crush their wine;
The nectarine and curious peach
Into my hands themselves do reach;
Stumbling on melons, as I pass
Ensnared with flowers, I fall on grass.

ANDREW MARVELL

FALLING ASLEEP

Voices moving about in the quiet house:
Thud of feet and a muffled shutting of doors:
Everyone yawning. Only the clocks are alert.

Out in the night there's autumn-smelling gloom
Crowded with whispering trees; across the park
A hollow cry of hounds like lonely bells:
And I know that the clouds are moving across the moon;
The low, red, rising moon. Now herons call
And wrangle by their pool; and hooting owls
Sail from the woods above pale stooks[†] of oats.

Waiting for sleep, I drift from thoughts like these;
And where to-day was dream-like, build my dreams.
Music . . . there was a bright white room below,
And someone singing a song about a soldier,
One hour, two hours ago; and soon the song
Will be *'last night'*: but now the beauty swings
Across my brain, ghost of remembered chords
Which still can make such radiance in my dream
That I can watch the marching of my soldiers,
And count their faces; faces; sunlit faces.

Falling asleep . . . the herons, and the hounds . . .
September in the darkness; and the world
I've known; all fading past me into peace.

SIEGFRIED SASSOON

[†]*shocks*

TO THE FRINGED GENTIAN

Thou blossom bright with autumn dew,
And coloured with the heaven's own blue,
That openest when the quiet light
Succeeds the keen and frosty night.

Thou comest not when violets lean
O'er wandering brooks and springs unseen,
Or columbines, in purple dressed,
Nod o'er the ground-bird's hidden nest;

Thou waitest late and com'st alone,
When woods are bare and birds are flown,
And frosts and shortening days portend
The aged year is near his end.

Then doth thy sweet and quiet eye
Look through its fringes to the sky,
Blue—-blue—as if that sky let fall
A flower from its cerulean wall.

I would that thus, when I shall see
The hour of death draw near to me,
Hope, blossoming within my heart,
May look to heaven as I depart.

WILLIAM CULLEN BRYANT

SEED-TIME

Flowers of the willow-herb are wool;
Flowers of the briar berries red;
Speeding their seed as the breeze may rule,
Flowers of the thistle loosen the thread.
Flowers of the clematis drip in beard,
Slack from the fir-tree youngly climbed;
Chaplets in air, flies foliage seared;
Heeled upon earth, lie clusters rimed.

Where were skies of the mantle stained
Orange and scarlet, a coat of frieze
Travels from North till day has waned,
Tattered, soaked in the ditch's dyes;
Tumbles the rook under grey or slate;
Else, enfolding us, damp to the bone;
Narrows the world to my neighbour's gate;
Paints me Life as a wheezy crone.

Now seems none but the spider's lord;
Star in circle his web waits prey,
Silvering bush-mounds, blue brushing sward;
Slow runs the hour, swift flits the ray.
Now to this thread-shroud is he nigh,
Nigh to the tangle where wings are sealed,
He who frolicked the jewelled fly;
All is adroop on the down† and the weald.‡

Mists more lone for the sheep-bell enwrap
Nights that tardily let slip a morn

†*hill*
‡*forest*

Paler than noons, and on noontide's lap
Flame dies cold, like the rose late born.
Rose born late, born withered in bud!—
I, even I, for a zenith of sun
Cry, to fulfil me, nourish my blood:
O for a day of the long light, one!

Master the blood, nor read by chills,
Earth admonishes: Hast thou ploughed,
Sown, reaped, harvested grain for the mills,
Thou hast the light over shadow of cloud.
Steadily eyeing, before that wail,
Animal infant, thy mind began,
Momently near me: should sight fail,
Plod in the track of the husbandman.

Verily now is our season of seed,
Now in our Autumn; and Earth discerns
Them that have served her in them that can read,
Glassing, where under the surface she burns,
Quick at her wheel, while the fuel, decay,
Brightens the fire of renewal: and we?
Death is the word of a bovine day,
Know you the breast of the springing To-be.

GEORGE MEREDITH

DIGGING

To-day I think
Only with scents,—scents dead leaves yield,
And bracken, and wild carrot's seed,
And the square mustard field;

Odours that rise
When the spade wounds the root of tree,
Rose, currant, raspberry, or goutweed,
Rhubarb or celery;

The smoke's smell, too,
Flowing from where a bonfire burns
The dead, the waste, the dangerous,
And all to sweetness turns.

It is enough
To smell, to crumble the dark earth,
While the robin sings over again
Sad songs of Autumn mirth.

EDWARD THOMAS

THE BURNING OF THE LEAVES

Now is the time for the burning of the leaves.
They go to the fire; the nostril pricks with smoke
Wandering slowly into a weeping mist.
Brittle and blotched, ragged and rotten sheaves!
A flame seizes the smouldering ruin and bites
On stubborn stalks that crackle as they resist.

The last hollyhock's fallen tower is dust;
All the spices of June are a bitter reek,
All the extravagant wishes spent and mean.
All burns! The reddest rose is a ghost;
Sparks whirl up, to expire in the mist: the wild
Fingers of fire are making corruption clean.

Now is the time for stripping the spirit bare,
Time for the burning of days ended and done,
Idle solace of things that have gone before:
Rootless hope and fruitless desire are there;
Let them go to the fire, with never a look behind.
The world that was ours is a world that is ours no more.

They will come again, the leaf and the flower, to arise
From squalor of rottenness into the old splendour,
And magical scents to a wondering memory bring;
The same glory, to shine upon different eyes.
Earth cares for her own ruins, naught for ours.
Nothing is certain, only the certain spring.

LAURENCE BINYON

THE WILD SWANS AT COOLE

The trees are in their autumn beauty,
The woodland paths are dry,
Under the October twilight the water
Mirrors a still sky;
Upon the brimming water among the stones
Are nine and fifty swans.

The nineteenth Autumn has come upon me
Since I first made my count;
I saw, before I had well finished,
All suddenly mount
And scatter wheeling in great broken rings
Upon their clamorous wings.

I have looked upon those brilliant creatures,
And now my heart is sore.
All's changed since I, hearing at twilight,
The first time on this shore,
The bell-beat of their wings above my head,
Trod with a lighter tread.

Unwearied still, lover by lover,
They paddle in the cold,
Companionable streams or climb the air;
Their hearts have not grown old;
Passion or conquest, wander where they will,
Attend upon them still.

But now they drift on the still water
Mysterious, beautiful;
Among what rushes will they build,
By what lake's edge or pool

Delight men's eyes when I awake some day
To find they have flown away?

WILLIAM BUTLER YEATS

POEM IN OCTOBER

It was my thirtieth year to heaven
Woke to my hearing from harbour and neighbour wood
    And the mussel pooled and the heron
        Priested shore
      The morning beckon
With water praying and call of seagull and rook
And the knack of sailing boats on the net webbed wall
      Myself to set foot
        That second
In the still sleeping town and set forth.

My birthday began with the water—
Birds and the birds of the winged trees flying my name
    Above the farms and the white horses
        And I rose
      In rainy autumn
And walked abroad in a shower of all my days.
High tide and the heron dived when I took the road
      Over the border
        And the gates
Of the town closed as the town awoke.

A springful of larks in a rolling

Cloud and the roadside bushes brimming with whistling
    Blackbirds and the sun of October
        Summery
      On the hill's shoulder
Here were fond climates and sweet singers suddenly
Come in the morning where I wandered and listened
      To the rain wringing
        Wind blow cold
    In the wood faraway under me.

    Pale rain in the dwindling harbour
And over the sea wet church the size of a snail
    With its horns through mist and the castle
        Brown as owls
      But all the gardens
Of spring and summer were blooming in the tall tales
Beyond the border and under the lark full cloud.
      There could I marvel
        My birthday
    Away but the weather turned around.

    It turned away from the blithe country
And down the other air and the blue altered sky
    Streamed again a wonder of summer
        With apples
      Pears and red currants
And I saw in the turning so clearly a child's
Forgotten morning when he walked with his mother
      Through the parables
        Of sunlight
    And the legends of the green chapels

    And the twice told fields of infancy

That his tears burned my cheeks and his heart moved in mine.
      These were the woods the river and sea
          Where a boy
        In the listening
Summertime of the dead whispered the truth of his joy
To the trees and the stones and the fish in the tide
      And the mystery
         Sang alive
Still in the water and singingbirds.

      And there I could marvel my birthday
Away but the weather turned around. And the true
      Joy of the long dead child sang burning
         In the sun.
      It was my thirtieth
Year to heaven stood there then in the summer noon
Though the town below lay leaved with October blood.
      O may my heart's truth
        Still be sung
On this high hill in a year's turning.

             DYLAN THOMAS

AUTUMN

Come! let us draw the curtains,
    heap up the fire and sit
hunched by the flame together,
    and make a friend of it.

Listen! the wind is rising,
    and the air is wild with leaves,
we have had our summer evenings:
    now for October eves!

The great beech-trees lean forward,
    and strip like a diver. We
had better turn to the fire,
    and shut our minds to the sea,

where the ships of youth are running
    close-hauled on the edge of the wind,
with all adventure before them,
    and only the old behind.

Love and youth and the seabirds
    meet in the stormy weather,
and with one bright flash of laughter
    clap in the dark together.

Come! let us draw the curtains,
    and talk of other things,
and presently all will be quiet—
    love, youth, and the sound of wings.

HUMBERT WOLFE

NORTH WIND IN OCTOBER

In the golden glade the chestnuts are fallen all;
From the sered boughs of the oak the acorns fall:
The beech scatters her ruddy fire;
The lime hath stripped to the cold,
And standeth naked above her yellow attire:
The larch thinneth her spire
To lay the ways of the wood with cloth of gold.

  Out of the golden-green and white
Of the brake the fir-trees stand upright
In the forest of flame, and wave aloft
To the blue of heaven their blue-green tuftings soft.

  But swiftly in shuddering gloom the splendours fail,
As the harrying North-wind beareth
A cloud of skirmishing hail
The grieved woodland to smite:
In a hurricane through the trees he teareth,
Raking the boughs and the leaves rending,
And whistleth to the descending
Blows of his icy flail.
Gold and snow he mixeth in spite,
And whirleth afar; as away on his winnowing flight
He passeth, and all again for awhile is bright.

ROBERT BRIDGES

SONNET

That time of year thou may'st in me behold
When yellow leaves, or none, or few, do hang
Upon those boughs which shake against the cold—
Bare ruin'd choirs where late the sweet birds sang.
In me thou see'st the twilight of such day
As after Sunset fadeth in the West,
Which by and by black night doth take away,
Death's second self, that seals up all in rest.
In me thou see'st the glowing of such fire
That on the ashes of his youth doth lie,
As the death-bed whereon it must expire,
Consumed with that which it was nourished by.
    This thou perceiv'st, which makes thy love more strong
    To love that well which thou must leave ere long.

WILLIAM SHAKESPEARE

FALL, LEAVES, FALL

Fall, leaves, fall; die, flowers, away;
Lengthen night and shorten day;
Every leaf speaks bliss to me
Fluttering from the autumn tree.
I shall smile when wreaths of snow
Blossom where the rose should grow;
I shall sing when night's decay
Ushers in a drearier day.

EMILY BRONTË

FROM **IN MEMORIAM**

To-night the winds begin to rise
    And roar from yonder dropping day:
    The last red leaf is whirl'd away,
The rooks are blown about the skies;

The forest crack'd, the waters curl'd,
    The cattle huddled on the lea;
    And wildly dash'd on tower and tree
The sunbeam strikes along the world:

And but for fancies which aver
    That all thy motions gently pass
    Athwart a plane of molten glass,
I scarce could brook the strain and stir

That makes the barren branches loud;
    And but for fear it is not so,
    The wild unrest that lives in woe
Would dote and pore on yonder cloud

That rises upward always higher,
    And onward drags a labouring breast,
    And topples round the dreary west,
A looming bastion fringed with fire.

ALFRED TENNYSON

NOVEMBER

Sybil of months, and worshipper of winds,
    I love thee, rude and boisterous as thou art;
And scraps of joy my wandering ever finds
    Mid thy uproarious madness—when the start
Of sudden tempests stirs the forest leaves
    Into hoarse fury, till the shower set free
Stills the huge swells. Then ebb the mighty heaves,
    That sway the forest like a troubled sea.
I love thy wizard noise, and rave in turn
    Half-vacant thoughts and rhymes of careless form;
Then hide me from the shower, a short sojourn,
    Neath ivied oak; and mutter to the storm,
Wishing its melody belonged to me,
That I might breathe a living song to thee.

                    JOHN CLARE

AUTUMN
A DIRGE

The warm sun is failing, the bleak wind is wailing,
The bare boughs are sighing, the pale flowers are dying,
          And the year
On the earth her deathbed, in a shroud of leaves dead
          Is lying.
          Come, months, come away,
          From November to May,
          In your saddest array;
          Follow the bier
          Of the dead cold year,
And like dim shadows watch by her sepulchre.

The chill rain is falling, the nipt worm is crawling,
The rivers are swelling, the thunder is knelling
          For the year;
The blithe swallows are flown, and the lizards each gone
          To his dwelling;
          Come, months, come away;
          Put on white, black, and grey,
          Let your light sisters play—
          Ye, follow the bier
          Of the dead cold year,
And make her grave green with tear on tear.

              PERCY BYSSHE SHELLEY

NOVEMBER

The mellow year is hastening to its close;
The little birds have almost sung their last,
Their small notes twitter in the dreary blast—
That shrill-piped harbinger of early snows;
The patient beauty of the scentless rose,
Oft with the Morn's hoar crystal quaintly glassed,
Hangs, a pale mourner for the summer past,
And makes a little summer where it grows:
In the chill sunbeam of the faint bright day
The dusky waters shudder as they shine,
The russet leaves obstruct the straggling way
Of oozy brooks, which no deep banks define,
And the gaunt woods, in ragged, scant array,
Wrap their old limbs with sombre ivy twine.

HARTLEY COLERIDGE

INDEX OF TITLES

INDEX OF AUTHORS

INDEX OF FIRST LINES